Questions AND Answers

KNIGHTS AND CASTLES

Philip Brooks

KINGFISHER

NEW YORK

KINGFISHER
Larousse Kingfisher Chambers Inc.
80 Maiden Lane
New York, New York 10038
www.kingfisherpub.com

Produced by Scintilla Editorial Ltd.

First published in 2001
10 9 8 7 6 5 4 3 2 1

1TR/0301/TIM/UNV/MA130

LIBRARY OF CONGRESS CATALOGING-IN-PUBLICATION DATA
has been applied for.

ISBN 0-7534-5371-1

Printed in China

Author: Philip Brooks
Editor: Fergus Collins
Art editor: Keith Davis
Designer: Joe Conneally

Illustrations: Francis D'Ohani, Kevin Toy, J. Gower,
G. D. Achille/Artist Partners, Martin Hargreaves, Nikki Palin,
Adam Hook, Angus McBride, Eddy Krähenbühl, Julian Baker,
Peter Dennis/Linda Rogers Agency, Ray Grinaway,
Lee Edwards, David McAllister/Simon Girling,
Shirley Tourret, Steiner Lund, Christa Hook/Linden Artists,
Nick Harris/Virgil Pomfret, John James

Contents

First Knights

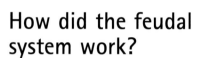

The king

Knights were noblemen who fought on horseback and often lived in castles. This lifestyle began in the early Middle Ages (see page 38) in France and spread across Europe. Knights were successful because they were part of a system that helped kings win wars and govern their kingdoms. It was known as the feudal system.

Roman cavalryman

Goth horseman

How did the feudal system work?

In a country with the feudal system, the king owned all the land, but he distributed some of the land to his lords, who were knights. This gift provided a knight with an income, but in return he had to fight for the king and help run the kingdom. In turn, the knight allowed peasants to make a living from his land, as long as they also worked for him.

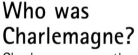

Who were the first knights?

Knights and feudalism arrived when Charlemagne (right) created his empire in the 800s. Earlier the Romans had used mounted soldiers, but their role in battle was limited. Some of the European peoples ruled by the Romans, such as the Celts and Goths, were good horsemen and fought on horseback. But they had no feudal system and so were not true knights.

Who was Charlemagne?

Charlemagne was the king of the Franks, a people who occupied France and western Germany. From his base at Aachen, he built up a huge empire. He set up local lords as governors of each area, giving them land in return for service—creating an early feudal system. In the year 800, he was given the title of Roman Emperor, although the true Roman Empire had fallen 300 years earlier.

Why were the Normans so powerful?

The Normans (left) were a people who originally came from Scandinavia and settled in northwestern France. They were good builders who erected many strong castles. Like their Viking ancestors, they were skilled soldiers, sailors, and boat builders. Unlike the Vikings, they also had a feudal system. All these factors helped them create a kingdom in France and England and rule it effectively. The Normans also carved out dominions in southern Italy and the Middle East.

What were mottes and baileys?

Mottes and baileys were the first true castles. When the Normans conquered England, they needed castles quickly as bases for their lords. They made a soil mound, called a motte, and built a wooden tower on top as a stronghold. Next to this they fenced off a yard, called a bailey, where they built a hall, stables, a chapel, and other buildings. A ditch or moat surrounded the castle.

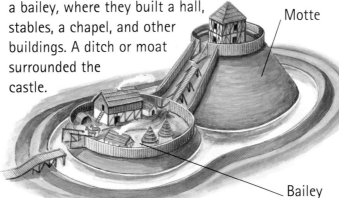

Motte

Bailey

How could you tell a high-ranking Norman?

A high-ranking Norman (above) rode a horse, carried a kite-shaped shield, and wore mail armor. He wielded a sword and a lance, and on his lance he tied a small flag, called a pennon, which showed he was a noble.

Were wooden castles weak?

Wooden castles were well protected by their mottes and moats, but they were easy to knock down or to attack with fire. Most of them were eventually replaced by stronger stone buildings.

Quick-fire Quiz

1. **What title was Charlemagne given in 800?**
a) Lord of the Franks
b) King of France
c) Roman Emperor

2. **Who were the Normans' ancestors?**
a) Vikings
b) Franks
c) Britons

3. **What did a Norman noble tie on his lance?**
a) A helmet
b) A handkerchief
c) A pennon

4. **What was a castle courtyard called?**
a) The motte
b) The bailey
c) The stronghold

Building a Castle

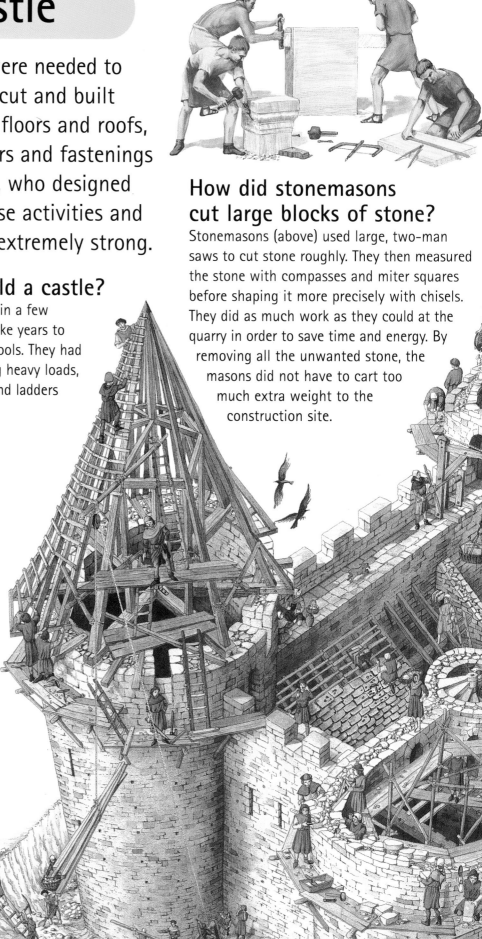

Many skilled craftsmen were needed to build a castle—masons cut and built with stone, carpenters made floors and roofs, and metalworkers shaped bars and fastenings for doors. The master mason, who designed the castle, supervised all these activities and made sure the building was extremely strong.

How long did it take to build a castle?

The Normans could finish a wooden castle in a few days, but a big stone castle (right) could take years to construct. Castle builders had no modern tools. They had to rely on simple aids like pulleys for lifting heavy loads, and they climbed up wooden scaffolding and ladders to reach the tops of high walls.

How did stonemasons cut large blocks of stone?

Stonemasons (above) used large, two-man saws to cut stone roughly. They then measured the stone with compasses and miter squares before shaping it more precisely with chisels. They did as much work as they could at the quarry in order to save time and energy. By removing all the unwanted stone, the masons did not have to cart too much extra weight to the construction site.

Why do the stairs spiral up to the right?

Coming down stairs going this way, a right-handed defender could easily use his weapon. An attacker coming up the stairs had less room to swing his sword.

How did they build the walls?

Castle builders liked to use neat, rectangular stone blocks shaped with a mallet and chisel for the walls—if they could get them. These would be bonded together tightly with cement (right) so that an attacker would find it difficult to break them down. Laid carefully, these blocks could even be used for the curves needed for round castle towers. For extra strength, rubble and cement were packed into the main walls (see page 9).

How did workers lift large stones?

Carrying heavy lumps of stone up to the castle battlements was hard work. Masons used a rope and pulley, linked to a simple wooden crank (left), to haul the stone into place. At the end of the rope they could attach a basket to carry small stones, or a pair of metal pincers to grip a larger block.

Why did they "turn" timber?

Carpenters used a tool called a lathe to make rounded items, like posts. Powered by a long, springy pole (right), the lathe could spin a piece of wood quickly. The carpenter held his chisel on the wood, removing the corners and giving it a round shape. This process is called turning.

How were planks cut from enormous tree trunks?

Medieval carpenters used a pit and a long, two-handled saw (above) to cut along the length of a tree trunk. One man stood inside the pit, pulling the saw down, while the other held the top end of the saw, guiding it carefully along. As they sawed, the workers drove wooden wedges into the gap to keep the cut open. One large trunk could make several planks.

Quick-fire Quiz

1. What gave the lathe its power?
a) A springy pole
b) A waterwheel
c) A motor

2. What was scaffolding made from?
a) Stone
b) Metal poles
c) Wooden poles

3. What did masons use to grip large stone blocks?
a) Hands
b) Metal pincers
c) Baskets

4. How many men usually worked at a saw pit?
a) One
b) Two
c) Three

Castle Designs

Castle builders tried all kinds of different designs to make their buildings stronger. One of the simplest was the square stone tower, or keep. But a keep was not enough on its own and was usually surrounded by extra walls. Later, builders added towers, gatehouses, and more walls.

Why were some towers round?

Round towers were stronger than square towers, because they did not have weak corners. In addition, defenders could fire arrows in many different directions from a round tower, giving them more chance of hitting their enemies. Not all towers were round, but their importance for defense made them increasingly popular.

What was a shell keep?

A shell keep was a circular stone wall on top of a soil mound. Many of these were built on the sites of old motte and bailey castles. Around the inside of a shell keep was a wall walk, where defenders could stand to shoot through the battlements. Below this were structures, such as the hall, built against the outer wall.

Why have extra sets of walls?

Early castles had just one set of walls. This made it fairly easy for an attacker to break inside, so builders began adding extra sets of walls (right). This slowed attackers down. It also meant that defenders could trap their enemies between two walls, making them sitting targets for defending archers.

Where was the castle strongest?

In early castles the stronghold was usually the keep. But when keeps went out of fashion, the gatehouse (above) became the strongest part. Gatehouses had thick walls, twin towers, and one or more strong gates, called portcullises (see page 27). Outside the main walls, lords sometimes built a barbican, a strong outer courtyard that an enemy would have to take before attacking the main castle.

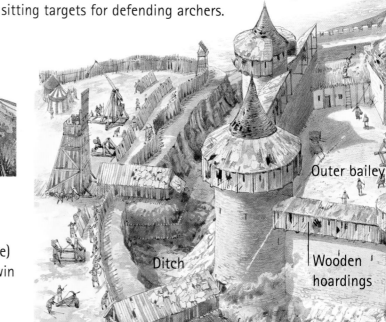

Outer bailey

Ditch

Wooden hoardings

How thick were the walls?

Stone castle walls could be several yards thick. The thicker they were, the harder they were for attackers to knock down. If they were really thick, enemies might not even try to attack them. Castle walls were actually two parallel walls with a gap between them. The gap could be filled with rubble to make them even stronger.

What was a concentric castle?

A concentric castle was a castle with two parallel sets of walls, one inside the other. As well as giving an enemy two barriers to get through, these twin walls provided defenders with two firing platforms. The outer wall was often lower than the one on the inside, so that one group of defending archers could fire safely over the heads of the others.

Chateau Gaillard (begun 1196)

Battlements

Keep

Inner wall

Inner bailey

Round tower

Outer wall

Quick-fire Quiz

1. Where did archers stand in a shell keep?
a) In the courtyard
b) On the wall walk
c) On the catwalk

2. Why did archers like round towers?
a) They gave more lines of fire
b) They were warm
c) They were spacious

3. What was a portcullis?
a) A type of tower
b) A strong gate
c) A thick wall

4. What were extra walls for?
a) To accommodate more soldiers
b) To prevent mining
c) For defense

Parts of the Castle

A castle had one or more courtyards, with main rooms in buildings along the insides of the courtyard walls. Near the great hall, where everyone ate, were the pantry and the kitchen. Stables, workshops, and extra living rooms were located in wall towers or in buildings separate from the great hall.

Where were the stables?

Stables were usually built in one of the castle courtyards. Like many buildings inside the walls, they could be large, but were often built of timber. Near the stables was a workshop for the farrier, the craftsman who made and fitted horseshoes.

What was in a keep?

Because the keep was one of the strongest parts of the castle, everything of value was kept in its basement. The lord's hall was above this, with the family's private rooms on the upper floor. Further floors were used by members of the lord's household.

Were dungeons really prisons?

The basement rooms in castle towers, now called dungeons, were storage rooms, not prisons. Weapons, equipment, and food would be kept here. Prisons were rare in the Middle Ages, and the only people held prisoner for long periods were nobles captured in battle. The nobles could then be set free in return for ransom—money (right) from their families.

Where was the bathroom?

Castles did not have bathrooms like those in modern houses. When people washed, they used a bowl of water. For toilets there were garderobes. A garderobe consisted of a wooden seat above a stone drain, which emptied through the castle wall directly into the moat. Garderobes smelled bad and must have been cold, because the drain usually led straight out into the open air.

How was the food cooked?

Castles had no modern kitchen appliances, so most food was cooked over the fire (left). The cook roasted meat on a spit, which could be turned with a handle so the food was cooked all around. Other foods were boiled in a large iron pot over the flames. Castle kitchens also had ovens for baking the bread that everyone ate with their meals.

Quick-fire Quiz

1. What was in the keep basement?
a) The hall
b) The storage room
c) The kitchen

2. What did a farrier make?
a) Castles
b) Horseshoes
c) Bread

3. Why might you be imprisoned?
a) For a minor crime
b) For a serious crime
c) For ransom

4. Why were garderobes cold?
a) They were used only in winter
b) They drained into the open air
c) They had large windows

How were wall towers used?

Wall towers (left) were used in all kinds of ways. Guards could get the best view of the surrounding country from the top of the stair turret and could fire at an enemy from the battlements around the roof. In the rooms below, there were more windows to shoot out from. In peacetime these rooms, which often had fireplaces, provided accommodation for the soldiers or members of the lord's family.

Did castles have gardens?

Many castles had gardens where vegetables and herbs were grown for cooking. In the later Middle Ages, when castles became more luxurious, some even had ornamental gardens. Here the flowers, herbs, shrubs, and trees were arranged in neat patterns.

Castle Life

During peacetime the lord and his followers collected rent from tenants and made sure the castle was in good repair. Knights went hunting to bring extra food for the table. Women and girls spun wool, cooked, and mended clothes. In the evening everyone came together for a meal in the great hall.

What kind of music entertained the guests?

Minstrels (right) played instruments and sang songs. The fiddle was popular, but after the Crusades many minstrels took up an Arab instrument, the lute. In Wales musicians played the harp, while the harplike psaltery was played all over Europe.

Where did everyone sleep?

Medieval castles had no bedrooms. The lord and his family usually slept in the solar (right), a private room next to the hall. Most of the rest of the household slept in the hall itself. After the evening meal they took down the tables and leaned them against the wall, then put straw-filled mattresses on the floor. Others slept where they worked. Cooks, for example, slept in the kitchen.

What was on the menu?

People ate whatever farmers could provide, plus what could be hunted. If food was plentiful, the diet included meat such as venison and boar together with beef, pork, and mutton from the farm. Bread and vegetables were served with the meat, often on a trencher—a dinner plate of firm bread. This was washed down with ale or wine (right). In lean times people ate meat preserved with salt and flavored with herbs to hide the salty taste.

Trencher

Did women have rights?

Medieval women had few rights. Few were educated, and most had to endure a life of household chores. If a woman had property, it passed to her husband when she died. For the lady of the manor, things could be different. She helped run the manor if her husband was away and might even have to defend the castle.

Who was the boss?

The lord was the boss, and everyone had to obey him. His power covered almost every aspect of life, from how his land should be farmed to who rode into battle with him. The only area that the lord did not control was religion—his power was second to that of the local bishop and clergy.

Who helped the lord?

A number of servants, from the steward to the reeve, helped run the lord's manor (see page 30). Others performed menial duties in the castle (above). Pages served at the lord's table, while grooms looked after his horses. He might have a clerk—who could also be the chaplain—to keep records and write letters. But the lord's constant companion and most important personal servant was his squire (see pages 14–15).

(see page 30)
(see pages 14–15)

Quick-fire Quiz

1. What was used to take away the saltiness of meat?
a) Dairy products
b) Herbs
c) Wines

2. Which musical instrument came from the Arab world?
a) Lute
b) Fiddle
c) Drum

3. How did people prevent drafts?
a) By building fires
b) By fitting carpets
c) By using tapestries

4. What were mattresses filled with?
a) Straw
b) Cotton
c) Springs

How did people keep warm?

Compared with houses today, castles and manor houses were cold and drafty, even when heated with blazing log fires. To keep down the drafts, the lords lined their walls with tapestries. People wore several layers of thick, wool clothing in the winter, and the rich added garments trimmed with fur (right) when the weather was really cold.

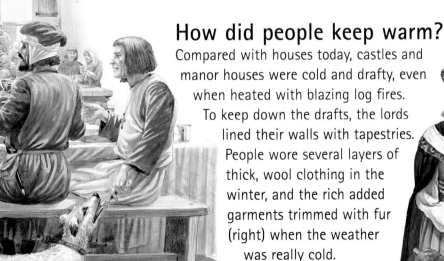

Becoming a Knight

To become a knight, a young man had to belong to a noble family. As a boy he began his training as a page and learned how to behave in a noble household. As a teenager he became a squire, learning knightly conduct and how to handle weapons and horses. Finally, in a ceremony known as dubbing, he became a knight.

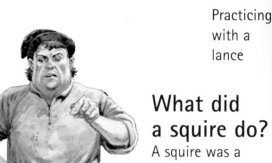

Serving at table

Practicing with a lance

How did a boy become a page?

If a boy was the son of a noble family, he did not go to school. Instead, when he was about seven years old, he was sent away to be a page in the household of another lord. Here he learned good manners and skills such as carrying food to the table (right) and serving his lord and lady.

What did a squire do?

A squire was a knight's personal servant and helper. His duties included looking after all the weapons and tending the horses. Before a battle the squire helped his master put on armor. He may even have had to fight beside his lord, providing aid if the knight was wounded. By doing all these things, a squire learned how to behave as a knight.

Did knights pray?

In the Middle Ages religion played a big part in most people's lives. When a squire was to be made a knight, he often spent the whole night before the dubbing ceremony in prayer in the castle chapel (left). This vigil was a sign that he would take his vows seriously to serve his king faithfully for the rest of his life.

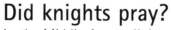
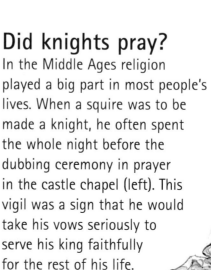

How did squires practice sword play?

For practice, knights and squires often used a sword and a small, round shield called a buckler. To build up strength, squires were sometimes given swords that were heavier than those actually used in battle. Pages or young squires might be given wooden swords to practice with.

Exercising

Helping the knight

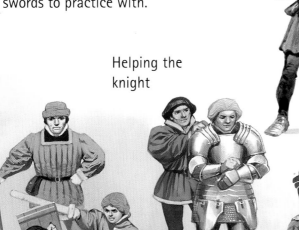

Practicing swordplay

Dubbing

How did squires exercise?

Squires kept in shape by practicing swordplay, wrestling, throwing the javelin, and all kinds of other sporting activities. They made sure that they were strong in case they had to go into battle.

Were knights and squires well-mannered?

Knights and squires were supposed to behave with good manners. They were meant to be considerate to women and courteous to all. But they did not always live up to this ideal. Sometimes squires got together in rowdy gangs and went around causing mischief. On one occasion they even burned down part of a town.

What was dubbing?

Dubbing was the ceremony at which a squire was made into a knight. The squire kneeled in front of his lord or the king, who tapped him on the shoulder with his sword. The new knight was then presented with a sword and spurs. There was often a celebration afterward.

Quick-fire Quiz

1. At what age did a boy become a page?
a) About four
b) About seven
c) About seventeen

2. Why could being a squire be dangerous?
a) Lords were cruel
b) You may have had to fight in battle
c) You had no shield

3. What was a small, round shield called?
a) A buckler
b) A helm
c) A hand shield

4. What was used to dub a knight?
a) A shield
b) A lance
c) A sword

Heraldry

In the Middle Ages every noble family had a coat of arms that acted as its badge. A knight wore his coat of arms into battle and when competing in a tournament so that he could be recognized easily. Coats of arms were always designed in a similar way, using the same range of colors and basic patterns.

 Groom's arms

 Bride's arms

Combined coat of arms

How was a coat of arms designed?

The herald chose the colors, shapes, and other designs that were suitable for the family who were to bear the arms. He made sure that the design was different from all others—every coat of arms had to be unique. When two noble families were united by marriage, the couple could have their two coats of arms combined (above), with the bride's and groom's arms on opposite sides of the shield.

What did heraldic symbols mean?

Many of the symbols used in heraldry have special meanings. Designs such as the diagonal bar (left) showed that the bearer's parents were not married. This was important in the Middle Ages, because an illegitimate son would not be able to inherit his father's title or lands.

What were a herald's duties?

A herald was an officer in the household of the king or great lord. As well as designing coats of arms (above), it was his job to organize ceremonies and tournaments. In war the herald carried messages between opposing armies (left). Therefore, it was essential that he could recognize every coat of arms, to deliver the message to the right person.

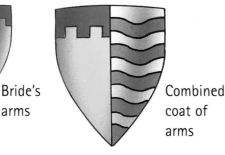

How could you recognize an eldest son?

An eldest son used his father's coat of arms, but with an added element. While the father was alive, the son's coat of arms was marked with a symbol called a label. The label ran across the shoulders and looked like a horizontal line with three thicker, downward-pointing lines joined to it. When the father died, the eldest son removed the label.

How were knights identified on the battlefield?

A knight's shield and his surcoat—a loose robe worn over the armor—were decorated with his coat of arms. This made it easy to see who was who in the confusion of battle. Heralds also used coats of arms to identify casualties after the battle (below).

Quick-fire Quiz

1. Which of these was a herald's job?
   a) Carrying messages
   b) Fighting
   c) Looking after the horses

2. Where were the supporters placed?
   a) Above the shield
   b) Below the shield
   c) On either side of the shield

3. What was red called in heraldry?
   a) Sable
   b) Scarlet
   c) Gules

4. What mark denoted an eldest son?
   a) Bar
   b) Label
   c) Chevron

What was the language of heraldry?

Coats of arms were described in a special language based on Old French. Each of the colors had its own name in this language—for example, red was called "gules," and black was referred to as "sable." Experts on heraldry still use this language to describe coats of arms today.

What were supporters?

The supporters were a pair of figures that stood on either side of the shield in a coat of arms, as if they were holding it up. These figures were often animals and could be real beasts, such as lions or antelope, or mythical ones, such as unicorns or griffons. Supporters were not normally shown on a knight's surcoat, but were included in the full coat of arms.

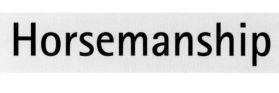

Horsemanship

Whether fighting, hunting, or traveling, a knight spent much of his time on horseback. A horse was the knight's most valued possession. As a page or squire he was shown how to ride and how to care for his mount. As he got older he learned how to fight on horseback using a sword and a lance so that he could fight for his king and take part in tournaments.

What was a destrier?

A destrier was a warhorse. Destriers were large, powerful stallions that could carry their owners swiftly into battle. The best and costliest destriers were said to come from southern Europe, especially from Italy and Spain. The name "destrier" comes from the Latin word for "right," perhaps because the horse led with its right leg, swerving away from an opponent in battle.

How many horses did a knight own?

Most knights had several horses, which were used for different tasks. A knight would have one or two warhorses (destriers), a powerful horse for hunting (a courser), and perhaps another one for traveling. Knights also kept packhorses in their stables. These were used to carry luggage when the knight and his household were traveling or when items had to be sent across the country.

How could you stop a horse in its tracks?

If footsoldiers were going into battle against mounted knights, they might scatter fearsome-looking, spiked objects called caltrops on the ground. A caltrop had four metal spikes, arranged so that whichever way the caltrop landed, one spike pointed up. A caltrop could injure a horse that stepped on it.

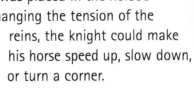

Caltrop

How did a knight control his horse?

A knight controlled his horse with both his feet and his hands. He placed his feet in a pair of stirrups and used them to grip his mount. This meant that the knight's hands were free to hold the reins or to wield a sword or a lance. The leather reins were connected to a bit that was placed in the horse's mouth. By changing the tension of the reins, the knight could make his horse speed up, slow down, or turn a corner.

Stirrup

Were spurs cruel?

A good rider would use his spurs only sparingly—for example, when urging his horse to give an extra burst of speed. Even so, a jab from the single, long, metal spike of a prick spur must have hurt; rowel spurs, with their rings of shorter spikes, did less damage.

Rowel spur

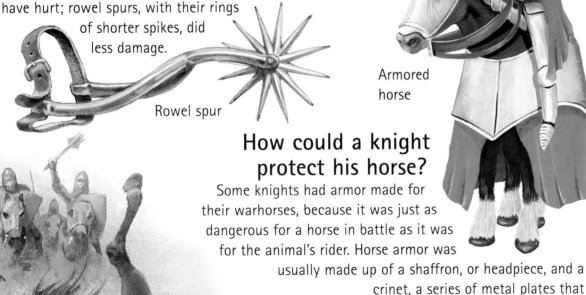

Armored horse

How could a knight protect his horse?

Some knights had armor made for their warhorses, because it was just as dangerous for a horse in battle as it was for the animal's rider. Horse armor was usually made up of a shaffron, or headpiece, and a crinet, a series of metal plates that covered the neck. Because plate armor was expensive, the rest of the horse sometimes went unprotected into battle.

Quick-fire Quiz

1. How many spikes did a prick spur have?
a) One
b Two
c) Three

2. What was a caltrop used for?
a) Killing soldiers
b) Controlling horses
c) Injuring horses

3. Where were the best warhorses bred?
a) Holland and Germany
b) Spain and Italy
c) Britain and Ireland

4. What was a knight's most valued possession?
a) His sword
b) His horse
c) His armor

Weapons and Fighting

The most feared sight on a medieval battlefield was a line of enemy knights charging directly at you. Well armored, mounted on warhorses, and wielding weapons that they had spent years training to use, knights were fast, powerful, and difficult to stop. A knight's favorite weapon was the sword, which could be used either on foot or from a horse, but he was adept with other weapons.

What was a double-edged sword used for?

A two-edged sword was used for cutting and slashing blows. This type of weapon was very effective against an enemy who was not wearing armor, especially if it was a "great sword" with a large grip that the knight could hold in both hands. He could then use all his strength to deliver powerful, cutting blows.

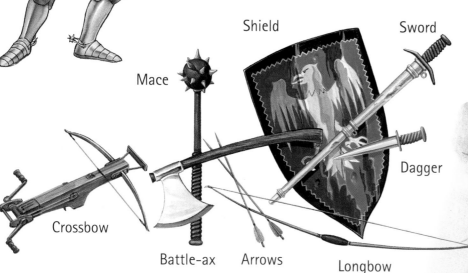

Mace

Shield

Sword

Dagger

Crossbow

Battle-ax   Arrows   Longbow

Did knights use only swords and daggers?

In addition to the sword, the knight used several other hand weapons (above and right), including the battle-ax and the mace. The mace was especially fearsome because its raised metal ridges or spikes concentrated the power of the blow, knocking the enemy sideways.

How did the Normans use their shields?

Norman soldiers held their large, kite-shaped shields in front of them to give plenty of protection. If a group of men was fighting in a row, they moved their shields together (below) to form a wall that archers or even mounted warriors found difficult to break through.

How did you use a flail?

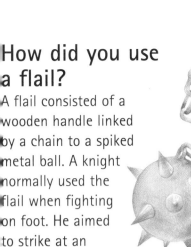

A flail consisted of a wooden handle linked by a chain to a spiked metal ball. A knight normally used the flail when fighting on foot. He aimed to strike at an enemy's head, knocking him out or piercing his armor.

How could you injure someone who was wearing mail?

To do serious injury to an opponent in mail (see page 22), a knight needed a sword or dagger with a narrow, sharp point, to get through one of the gaps between the metal rings. Archers (right) also found that they could pierce mail by using narrow metal heads on their arrows.

When was a lance used?

A lance was a long, heavy, polelike weapon, which was most effective at the start of a battle. Wielded by mounted knights charging swiftly, it could kill a man with a single thrust. After the charge, the knight discarded the lance and drew his sword—a better weapon for one-on-one fighting.

How were swords made stronger?

Armorers gave blades extra strength by altering their shape. A blade with a cross section like an elongated diamond was the strongest. Both cutting and stabbing swords (below) were made with blades in this shape.

Quick-fire Quiz

1. How did you hold a "great sword"?
a) Close to the chest
b) With one hand
c) With two hands

2. Which blade shape gave greatest strength?
a) Diamond
b) Rounded
c) Hollow

3. What did a weapon need to pierce mail?
a) A narrow point
b) Extra power
c) Plenty of weight

4. Where was a knight most likely to use a flail?
a) On horseback
b) On foot
c) In a boat

Armor

Every knight wanted to go into battle well protected. In the early Middle Ages knights wore mail, but armor made up of metal plates became more popular. Knights liked plate armor because it protected them well from arrows and sword blows, while allowing them to move with great freedom. But only a rich man could afford a full suit of plate armor.

How could you "knit" with metal?

By making mail. Mail, or chain mail as it is sometimes called, was a form of armor made up of thousands of tiny, linked metal rings. By varying the number of rings in a row, the armorer could shape mail into garments such as shirts, head coverings, leg guards, and even mittens. Mail was popular until plate armor became fashionable in the late 1200s.

Single ring

Linked mail

What did the armorer do?

Armorers (below) were skilled craftsmen who made both armor and weapons and could beat pieces of metal into sturdy breastplates or helmets. They did this by hammering a sheet of metal on an anvil or on a rounded object called a former. This gave the piece the right curve. Suits of armor often came back damaged from battle, so armorers also spent a lot of time on repairs.

Conical helmet

Basinet

Great helm (jousting)

Frog-mouthed (jousting)

Barbute

Why were there so many types of helmets?

Fashions in helmets changed just like fashions in clothes. In the late 1300s knights often wore the basinet, a helmet with a pointed visor and a collar of mail, which offered excellent protection. By the mid-1400s, they were wearing lighter helmets, called barbutes. For jousts and tournaments a rich knight might wear a highly decorated great helm.

What did a knight wear under his armor?

Under his armor a knight wore a padded jacket called an arming doublet. The doublet had sections of mail sewn under the arms and in other places to protect areas where there were gaps between the plates.

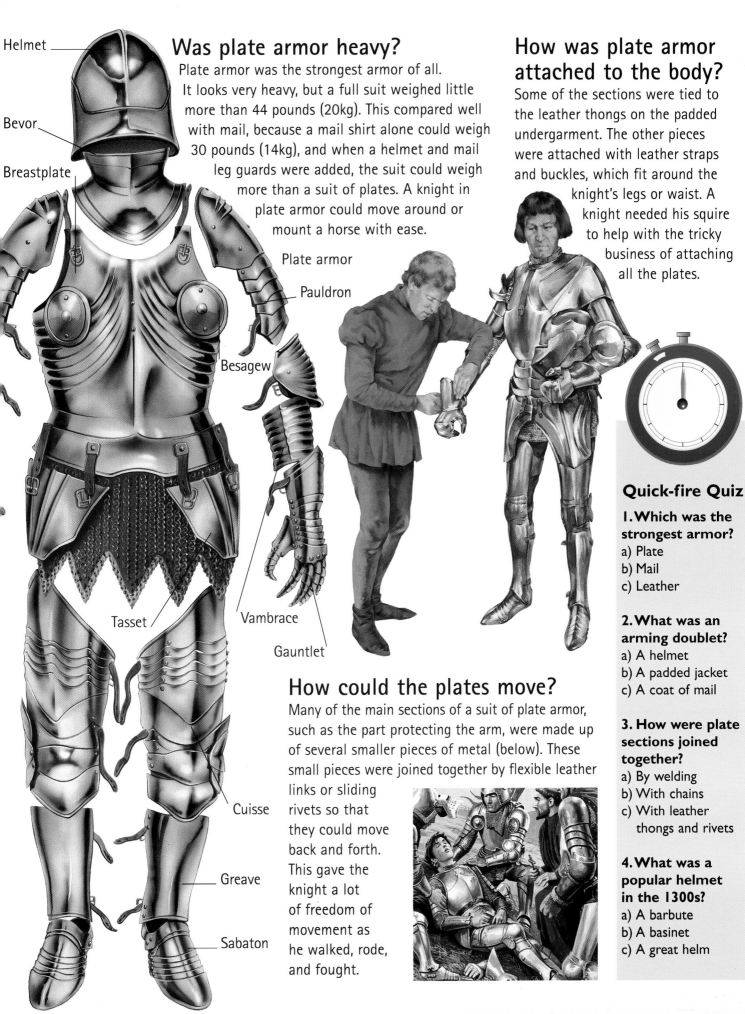

Helmet

Bevor

Breastplate

Plate armor

Pauldron

Besagew

Tasset

Vambrace

Gauntlet

Cuisse

Greave

Sabaton

Was plate armor heavy?

Plate armor was the strongest armor of all. It looks very heavy, but a full suit weighed little more than 44 pounds (20kg). This compared well with mail, because a mail shirt alone could weigh 30 pounds (14kg), and when a helmet and mail leg guards were added, the suit could weigh more than a suit of plates. A knight in plate armor could move around or mount a horse with ease.

How was plate armor attached to the body?

Some of the sections were tied to the leather thongs on the padded undergarment. The other pieces were attached with leather straps and buckles, which fit around the knight's legs or waist. A knight needed his squire to help with the tricky business of attaching all the plates.

How could the plates move?

Many of the main sections of a suit of plate armor, such as the part protecting the arm, were made up of several smaller pieces of metal (below). These small pieces were joined together by flexible leather links or sliding rivets so that they could move back and forth. This gave the knight a lot of freedom of movement as he walked, rode, and fought.

Quick-fire Quiz

1. Which was the strongest armor?
a) Plate
b) Mail
c) Leather

2. What was an arming doublet?
a) A helmet
b) A padded jacket
c) A coat of mail

3. How were plate sections joined together?
a) By welding
b) With chains
c) With leather thongs and rivets

4. What was a popular helmet in the 1300s?
a) A barbute
b) A basinet
c) A great helm

Siege

When enemy forces arrived to attack a castle, the castle's owner and his men pulled up the drawbridge and got ready for a siege. The siege could end peacefully, especially if the defenders ran out of food and were forced to surrender. But if there was a fight, the attackers could use all kinds of powerful weapons to force their way in.

How effective were archers?

The longbow was one of the medieval soldier's most awesome weapons. Its deadly arrows could fly almost 1,000 feet (300m), and a skilled archer could fire up to 12 arrows a minute. Castle defenders had to hide behind the battlements to avoid the arrows' sharp metal points.

What were siege engines?

The devices used by medieval armies to attack castles were known as siege engines. They were fearsome weapons that hurled missiles at the enemy or knocked down walls. The trebuchet and the mangonel were catapults powerful enough to fling heavy rocks. The ballista, a giant crossbow, shot bolts that were often tipped with blazing rags. Weapons on wheeled platforms could be moved into position to find their target. Reloading very large devices was slow work, but their devastating power struck fear into the enemy.

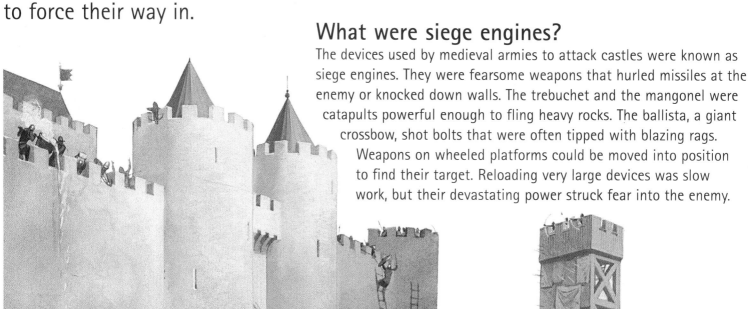

Mangonel

How could an attacker get through walls?

One way was to batter down the walls using a ram, a huge tree trunk mounted on wheels. A group of men, protected by the ram's roof, struck the walls repeatedly with the ram until they toppled. Alternatively, attackers could try wheeling a wooden siege tower up to the walls and climbing over. Both the ram and the tower were covered with animal skins to protect their wooden structures from flaming arrows.

Siege tower

Ram

What was mining?

Mining was another way of bringing down castle walls. The miners dug a tunnel under the walls, using wooden props to keep the tunnel from collapsing. Once they finished digging, they lit a fire in the tunnel. This set the props alight, so that the walls above no longer had anything to support them. If all went according to plan, a section of the castle walls collapsed, and the attackers swarmed into the castle. If the defenders saw a mine being dug, however, they could retaliate by digging their own tunnel into the mine and fighting off the attackers.

Tunnel entrance, far away from the walls

Miners set fire to wooden props

Workers bring wood for the fire

Soldiers remove vital foundation rocks

Trebuchet

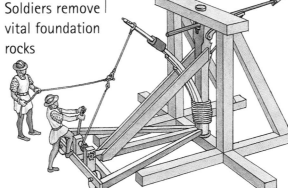

How did a catapult work?

Catapults worked like giant slings to launch missiles at or over walls. Trebuchets used counterweights; the mangonel's sling was held by ropes, which were then released. It took many men to reload the largest catapults.

Quick-fire Quiz

1. What were siege towers covered with?
a) Wood
b) Animal skins
c) Turf

2. How fast could an archer shoot?
a) 2 times a minute
b) 12 times a minute
c) 22 times a minute

3. How did miners hold up a tunnel?
a) With stone pillars
b) With their hands
c) With wooden props

4. What was a trebuchet for?
a) To break down castle walls
b) To hurl missiles at the enemy
c) To enable attackers to scale walls

Defense

Everything about a castle was designed to make it easy to defend. The walls were thick to withstand attacks from siege engines, while windows were small to keep out arrows. Battlements, towers, and hoardings all gave good lines of fire.

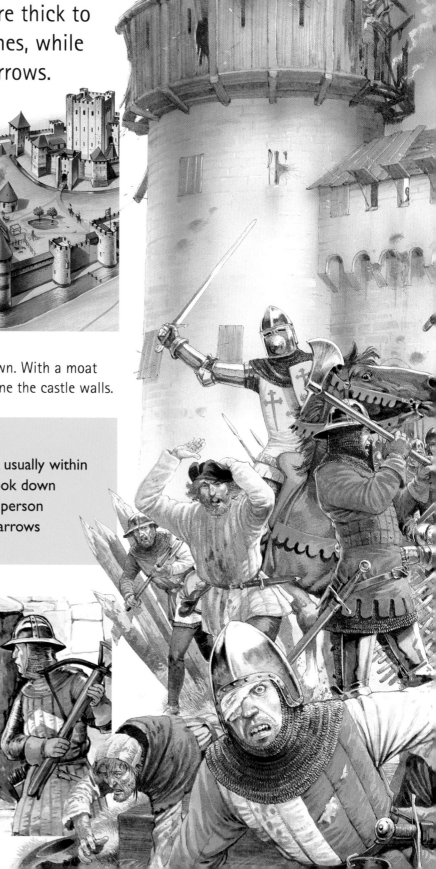

What was a moat?

A moat was a barrier between the castle and its attackers. Many castles were surrounded by dry ditches, but a water-filled moat gave more protection. An attacker could walk across a dry ditch and start mining— digging holes under the walls to make them fall down. With a moat it was virtually impossible for the enemy to undermine the castle walls.

What were murder holes?

Murder holes were small openings in the ceiling, usually within a castle gatehouse. They enabled defenders to look down at anyone passing through the gate below. If the person below was an enemy, the defender could shoot arrows or pour boiling liquid through one of the holes.

How was an embrasure used?

An embrasure was a hole in the wall where an archer could stand. The hole was splayed on the inside so that the archer could stand to one side of the opening, out of reach of enemy fire. When the archer was ready to shoot, he moved quickly to the opening, fired his arrow, and then ducked back out of range.

How could you pour boiling oil on your enemies?

Castle defenders sometimes emptied boiling oil or water straight over the battlements onto their enemies below. Another method was to use the machicolations, which were holes in the floor right next to the battlements. Anything poured through these would land on an opponent who was attacking the base of the wall or trying to climb it.

How did you make a sortie?

To make a sortie (left), defenders left the safety of the castle and launched an attack on the besieging enemy. The defenders burst out, trying to take their enemies by surprise before the walls of their stronghold were destroyed. A sortie would often target the powerful siege engines and their trained crews.

What were hoardings?

Wooden hoardings (right) were often built over the battlements to protect archers while providing them with a wide field of fire. Sometimes hoardings also had holes in the floor, for pouring boiling oil or firing at attackers directly below.

What was a portcullis?

A portcullis was a barred gate controlled by ropes and pulleys. It was closed by dropping it down from above. If a portcullis was dropped down on an enemy, he could be caught between its spiked bars (right).

Quick-fire Quiz

1. Where would you find murder holes?
a) In the walls
b) In the ceiling
c) In the battlements

2. How were machicolations used?
a) For ventilation
b) For letting in light
c) For pouring boiling oil on attackers

3. What material were hoardings made from?
a) Wood
b) Leather
c) Stone

4. What could a moat prevent?
a) Mining
b) Arrows
c) Sorties

The Crusades

In the late 1000s Christian rulers tried to take control of the Holy Land—the part of the Middle East where Jesus had lived. At that time the Holy Land was ruled by the Muslims—followers of Islam—to whom the area was also sacred. It was the start of a bitter conflict—the Crusades.

Who went on the Crusades?

All kinds of people went on the Crusades. Some were kings, such as Richard I of England and Philip II of France. Others were nobles, and many were men-at-arms who went with their lords to the east. A large number of poor peasants also went on crusade, inspired by leaders such as the French monk Peter the Hermit.

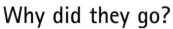

Why did they go?

Many crusaders were men who genuinely believed that it was right to fight for control of the Christian sites in the Holy Land. But others went just for the adventure or because they thought that they could benefit, either by looting after battles or by setting themselves up as lords in the east. Many of the latter were the younger sons of nobles, who would not inherit any of their parents' wealth back home.

What was the Children's Crusade?

In 1212 Nicholas, a 12-year-old boy from Cologne, Germany, led thousands of children across the Alps and into Italy on their way to the Holy Land. Another boy, Stephen, from France, led another group of children. Both groups failed. Stephen and his followers were captured and sold as slaves; the followers of Nicholas died in Italy.

Who were the "fighting monks"?

The fighting monks were groups of men who took religious vows but were still allowed to fight the Muslims. There were several groups, or orders, of fighting monks—the Knights Templar (named after their headquarters near the Temple in Jerusalem), the Knights of St. John (famous for their work healing the sick), and the Teutonic Knights (who originally came from Germany).

What did the Crusades achieve?

Although the crusaders set up states in the Middle East, these were soon reconquered. Only the ruins of their great castles, such as Krak des Chevaliers (below), survive. But they brought useful knowledge back to Europe, as well as new medicines and eastern inventions such as the windmill.

Who was Saladin?

Saladin was a Muslim leader in the 1100s who ruled Egypt and part of Syria. He defended his lands from crusaders and defeated the Second Crusade. When the Third Crusade began, Saladin fought Richard I of England. Again Saladin was victorious and greatly reduced the crusaders' power.

Saladin

How many crusades were there?

There were eight separate crusades from Europe to the Holy Land between the 1000s and the 1200s. The most successful was the first (1096–99), which was led by a group of French and Norman barons. It ended with the capture of Jerusalem. In 1271 the last crusader territory in the Holy Land was lost to the Muslims.

Quick-fire Quiz

1. Which French king led a crusade?
a) Philip I
b) Philip II
c) Richard I

2. Who led the First Crusade?
a) French and Norman barons
b) Richard I
c) German lords

3. Which was the most successful crusade?
a) The fourth
b) The second
c) The first

4. What were the Knights of St. John known for?
a) Healing the sick
b) Helping the poor
c) Fighting for St. John

The Knight's Manor

A manor consisted of a lord's castle, church, houses for the peasants, and farmland. The lord was the most important person. He was the landlord, boss, and judge, and the peasants had to do what he told them. These peasants were known as serfs or villeins; they had no freedom.

Who looked after the money?

The person who kept the accounts on the manor was the steward (left). He had to be educated, although most accounting systems were primitive. Later a group of merchants in Italy invented the system of double-entry bookkeeping, which is still used by accountants today. As well as looking after the money, the steward managed the lord's farm and also acted as judge in the manorial court if the lord was away.

What did the bailiff do?

The bailiff was a peasant farmer who had his own land. As well as his own fields, he looked after the day-to-day running of the lord's personal land, making sure that all the jobs were done correctly and at the right time. In addition, the bailiff was responsible for repairs and building work on the manor, bringing in any workers, such as stonemasons or carpenters, to get these jobs done. He was second in importance to the steward.

What was life like for the workers?

Life was hard for peasants. Men spent nearly all their time working in the fields. Women had to cook, look after the house, and make the family's clothes. For children there was no school. Boys helped in the fields while girls learned how to spin, sew, and cook.

Sunday and religious holidays were the only days off. For some, local markets (below) offered a welcome break from the hardships of daily life.

Who kept watch on the peasants?

The reeve (right) was the person who kept an eye on the peasants. He was a peasant himself, chosen by his peers, and he worked closely with the bailiff. He was most often seen out in the fields, making sure that everyone was working hard. But if any of the workers had a problem, the reeve could tell the bailiff, who would then decide what to do or whether to report the matter to the lord.

Reeve

Quick-fire Quiz

1. Who was judge in the court when the lord was away?
a) The bailiff
b) The reeve
c) The steward

2. Who farmed the demesne?
a) The lord
b) The sheriff
c) The reeve

3. How many years did a peasant spend at school?
a) Ten
b) Six
c) None

4. What caused so many women to die young?
a) Overwork
b) Black Death
c) Childbirth

Who worked the lord's land?

The lord's land was divided into two sections. Most was allotted to the peasants, who were allowed to work the land in return for services to the lord and a share of the produce. The rest of the lord's land was called the demesne. This was farmed by the lord with help from the peasants, who owed him some of their labor each week.

Who dealt with criminals?

The lord held his own court in his hall for minor crimes. Punishments included whipping, beating, fines, or being locked in the stocks. Serious offenses were judged by the county sheriff and could be punished by death by hanging. The church had its own laws and courts (above) for dealing with lawbreakers among the clergy.

What happened when people were sick?

Medieval medicine was basic. Some herbal medicines worked well, but other remedies, such as bloodletting, did no good. As a result, many people died of minor illnesses, and few lived beyond the age of 40. Life was especially hard for women, many of whom died in childbirth. The most feared illness was the bubonic plague, or the Black Death (right). It killed a third of the population of Europe in the 1300s.

Peacetime Pursuits

In the Middle Ages people had to create their own entertainment. Poor families filled their limited spare time with simple games and storytelling. For noble families, life was easier, but even knights had to mix some of their pleasure with work. Many liked to hunt, but the main reason for hunting was to provide food.

What were pastimes for adults?

Some people liked to play board games, such as chess (above), which appealed to noblemen because it is like a battle. Otherwise, knights and their ladies looked forward to visits from musicians and actors who arrived from time to time and performed in return for board and lodging.

What was chivalry?

Chivalry was a code of conduct that all knights were supposed to follow. A knight was expected to be considerate, especially toward women, and to treat enemies with respect. Many did not live up to this, but the Middle Ages are often known as the "Age of Chivalry."

What were the favorite games?

Peasant children usually played games, such as leapfrog and tag, that did not need any equipment, since ordinary families could not afford toys. Noble families had more money, and a knight's children were sometimes given toys, such as wooden swords and shields or miniature models of men-at-arms.

How did a falconer exercise his birds?

Falconers trained their birds to hunt and bring back prey. One way to exercise a falcon was to let it hunt for animals as it would in the wild. An alternative was to use a lure—a fake bird on the end of a long string. The falconer twirled the lure around in the air, encouraging the bird to pounce on it.

Why did girls learn to spin?

In the Middle Ages most manors kept sheep for meat and for wool. It was the job of the women and girls to spin the wool into yarn, which was then woven into cloth. A simple spindle or wooden spinning wheel was all that was needed, so almost every medieval girl learned to spin to produce yarn.

How did people like to be entertained?

One of the favorite pastimes was telling stories. Few people could read, but popular tales were handed down from one generation to the next by word of mouth. People liked to listen to stories about the exploits and loves of knights in times gone by. Some of the favorites were about the adventures of the mythical English king Arthur (right) and his Knights of the Round Table.

Which creatures did knights most enjoy hunting?

Knights hunted animals that they could eat. They liked to chase large creatures that provided plenty of meat—and offered a challenge to the hunter. Deer and wild boar were favorites. When these animals were scarce, smaller creatures like hares were hunted. Poorer people might have hunted birds or rabbits. In the Middle Ages there were few imported foods, and everyone had to eat what could be grown on the local land. Hunting made the diet more varied. Hunting also offered knights useful riding practice for war.

Quick-fire Quiz

1. What animals did knights hunt?
   a) Falcons
   b) Dogs
   c) Deer

2. Which king was a favorite of storytellers?
   a) King Alfred
   b) King Arthur
   c) King Albert

3. What are the Middle Ages sometimes called?
   a) Age of Innocence
   b) Age of Chivalry
   c) Bronze Age

4. Which board game was popular with noblemen?
   a) Chess
   b) Checkers
   c) Solitaire

Tournaments

Knights needed to practice fighting, so they often engaged in mock combat as a rehearsal for war. Many people liked to watch the knights fight, so tournaments soon became great festivals to which spectators came from far and wide. As well as mock battles, knights also fought one-to-one on horseback in the joust and with swords in foot combat.

What happened in a joust?

In a joust (right) two mounted knights hurtled toward each other and tried to knock each other off their horses as they passed. The weapon they used was the lance—either a pointed lance for the "joust of war," or a safer, blunt lance for the "joust of peace." Both types of jousts were stunning spectacles. Knights wore special armor for the joust. Their breastplates had metal rests for their lances, and they wore helmets that covered the entire head. Only a narrow slit was left in the helmet to allow the knight to see his target.

How did squires practice for the joust?

Jousting was dangerous, so knights invented a safer way to practice. Squires rode toward a quintain, a device with two moving arms attached to a wooden post. One arm held a shield, the other a heavy weight. The squire had to hit the shield with his lance, then ride past swiftly to avoid being hit by the swinging weight, which quickly spun around at him.

What if you weren't a knight?

Men who were not knights could train for war by practicing archery. Archers organized competitions, with everyone trying to hit the gold circle in the center of the target. To protect spectators, there was a barrier or a mound of soil, called the butts, behind the targets.

What drew spectators to the tournament?

Many people liked the pageantry seen at the tournament. This included the knights' shields decorated with their coats of arms, the banners, and the brightly patterned cloths—called caparisons—on the horses. As the knights rode through the streets to the tournament, onlookers could easily recognize those they supported from all the badges and heraldry.

Quick-fire Quiz

1. Which of these could be found on a quintain?
a) A helmet
b) A sword
c) A shield

2. Which weapon was used in a joust?
a) The sword
b) The lance
c) The mace

3. Who took part in tournaments?
a) Knights
b) Squires
c) Common soldiers

4. In archery, what was the mound of soil behind the targets called?
a) The knoll
b) The butts
c) The bumps

Who took part in tournaments?

It was mostly knights who took part, and they were usually members of the country's powerful families. Large-scale mock battles, called melees (right), involved many knights, and sometimes foot soldiers too. Tournaments were hosted by the king or one of his highest-ranking lords. As well as giving battle practice, tournaments showed people how strong the king was and how many knightly followers he had.

The Last Castles

After the 1400s nobles stopped building castles as secure strongholds. Instead they built elegant houses in which to enjoy a life of comfort. This came about because of changes in the way nobles lived and how battles were fought. Some families still lived in buildings that looked like castles from the outside, but would have been of little use in war.

Were cannons effective against castles?

The first cannons (above), used from the 1300s onward, did not always work very well. They made a lot of noise, but damaged few castles. But as time went on, cannons became larger and more reliable and could blow huge holes in castle walls. This meant that, by the 1500s, castles were no longer as secure from attack as they had been.

Was armor bullet-proof?

Yes. Armorers normally tried to make their plates thick enough to stop a bullet. As firearms became more common from the 1400s, people were anxious to be protected by their armor. Armorers often fired bullets at their breastplates before the armor left the workshop. The mark left by the bullet reassured the wearer that he would be safe.

How did leather replace armor?

By the 1600s light cavalry soldiers (left) were doing the jobs of knights on the battlefield. Many of these horsemen found that a jacket of pale leather—called a buff coat— gave them enough protection from sword cuts. Buff coats were worn with a metal breastplate and helmet, to shield the most vulnerable parts of the body.

Why did knights stop building castles?

In 1453 the Ottoman Turks laid siege to Constantinople (modern Istanbul), the capital of the Byzantine Empire (left). When their firearms battered down the walls and the Turks swarmed into the great city, it seemed to be the end of an era. Lords realized that there was little point in building stone castles for defense. At the same time the feudal system was breaking down. Knights were no longer powerful, and other people—especially merchants— were getting richer. The age of castles was at an end.

Are there new castles?

Many nobles in the late 1700s and 1800s wanted to revive the Age of Chivalry. They designed their homes in the style of castles by adding towers, gatehouses, thick walls, and pointed windows, to create buildings like Schloss Neuschwanstein in Germany (above).

Why are so many castles ruined?

A castle could be damaged in a siege or "slighted" by an enemy to make it unusable. Some lords abandoned their castles because they wanted a more comfortable home. Local people would use much of the stone to build new houses.

How did castles change?

Lords still lived in castles after the 1400s, but these castles were no longer built to withstand a siege. Nobles added features that gave them more comfort, such as luxurious bedrooms. Inside walls were lined with wooden paneling, and decorated plasterwork adorned the ceilings. Castle owners also put in bigger windows, so the rooms were much more light and airy than in medieval castles.

Quick-fire Quiz

1. Who might wear a buff coat?
a) The lady of the manor
b) A squire
c) A cavalry soldier

2. How did armorers test plate armor?
a) By firing bullets at it
b) By hammering it
c) By heating it

3. How did castle windows change over the centuries?
a) They got smaller
b) They got bigger
c) They were filled in

4. Which weapon was the greatest threat to castles?
a) Siege tower
b) Cannon
c) Catapult

Timeline

This timeline records the key dates in the history of castles and knights. Most of the story takes place in a period known as the Middle Ages, or the medieval era. This period is called the "Middle" Ages because it is midway between the end of the Roman Empire (in the 400s) and the Renaissance (in the 1400s). The period does not have precise dates, but many historians say that the Middle Ages lasted from 500 to 1500.

A.D. 1 to 800

1–500 Romans use light cavalry troops to support footsoldiers. They build forts throughout Europe to defend their empire.

350–550 Western Roman Empire disintegrates.

410 Goths sack Rome.

622 The Islamic religion is established.

634 Omar I, caliph of the Arab Muslims, conquers Holy Land from Byzantines.

771 Charlemagne becomes king of the Franks. He uses mounted warriors to defend his lands.

790s Vikings begin raids on Britain and mainland Europe.

800 to 1000

800 Charlemagne is crowned Holy Roman Emperor by Pope Leo III.

800–1000 Rulers in western Europe begin to grant land to their nobles in return for services—the feudal system is established.

800–1150 The current style of architecture is the Romanesque, featuring rounded arches, thick walls, and tunnellike barrel vaults.

911 The Viking leader Rollo settles with his followers in northwestern France. They become known as the Normans, and their territory Normandy.

950 The stone keep at Doué-la-Fontaine, France, is built. This is now the oldest stone keep to survive.

987–1040 Foulques Nerra of Anjou builds 27 castles as part of his war with the Count of Blois.

1000 to 1100

1000 The Normans spread the fashion for castle-building around many areas of Europe. They begin by building wooden motte-and-bailey castles, but later construct castles using stone.

1000–1200 Many Italian towns become independent states, each defended by its own stone walls and castle. Italian lords each build their own stone tower, and some cities have many towers, with lords competing to build the tallest.

1066 William of Normandy invades England and defeats King Harold II at the Battle of Hastings. As his nobles take over they build castles all over the country to increase their power.

1071 William of Poitiers, said to be the first troubadour (medieval poet and singer), is born.

1090 Christian writers lay down rules of conduct for knights. The rules become the code of chivalry.

1095 Pope Urban II preaches the First Crusade.

1096–99 The First Crusade. Jerusalem is captured from the Muslims.

1100 Tower keeps become popular in many areas. In England and France stocky, square towers are common; German knights prefer more slender towers surrounded by strong curtain walls.

1100 to 1200

1100–1200 Many crusader castles are built.
1113 The Knights of St. John are founded in Jerusalem.
1118 The Knights Templar build their first headquarters near the Temple in Jerusalem.
1142 Crusaders take and rebuild Syria's greatest castle, the Krak des Chevaliers.
1147–49 The Second Crusade.
1150 The Gothic style replaces the Romaneqsue as the favored building style.
1160 Castle builders experiment with differently shaped keeps. Round keeps and many-sided designs are tried.
1170 Many Norman mottes with wooden towers are converted into stone shell keeps.
1180 Philip Augustus, one of the greatest French kings, comes to the throne; he will build many castles in his kingdom.
1188–92 The Third Crusade.
1190 The Teutonic Knights are founded. They build many castles in Europe.
1190 The keep goes out of fashion. Builders concentrate on courtyard castles with strong gatehouses.
1196 Richard I begins work on Château Gaillard, France. One of the strongest castles, it will withstand a siege for over a year.

1200 to 1300

1200 Rounded wall towers become popular.
1202–04 The Fourth Crusade.
1212 The Children's Crusade.
1217–22 The Fifth Crusade.
1228–29 The Sixth Crusade.
1220 Frederick II, one of the greatest castle builders, becomes Holy Roman Emperor.
1248–54 The Seventh Crusade.
1270 Rise of the concentric castle.
1270 The Eighth Crusade.
1272 Edward I comes to the throne of England. He launches military campaigns against the Scots and Welsh and builds many castles to control the population.
1291 Sultan Baybars storms the Christian city of Acre, and the crusading movement comes to an end.

1300 to 1400

1302 Battle of Courtrai. Flemish peasants armed with pikes defeat mounted French knights, proving that knights are not invincible in battle.
1312 The Knights Templar are dissolved.
1320s Cannons are first used in Europe.
1330 Plate armor becomes more fashionable.
1337–1453 The Hundred Years' War between England and France.
1347–51 The Black Death kills around one third of the population of Europe.
1380 Castle builders start to use gun loops so that defenders can fire out safely.

1400 to 1600

1400 Decline of castles begins.
1415 Battle of Agincourt. Henry V of England defeats army of French knights.
1450 Thicker walls are built to protect castles from pounding by cannon.
1453 The city of Constantinople, capital of the Byzantine Empire, falls to the Ottoman Turks, ending the Byzantine Empire.
1476–77 France fights wars with the Duchy of Burgundy; the widespread use of pikes and handguns shows that the age of the knight is coming to an end.
1500s Lords convert their castles into more comfortable residences or build palaces.
1509 Henry VIII builds forts (strongholds designed for guns where no one lives permanently) rather than true castles.

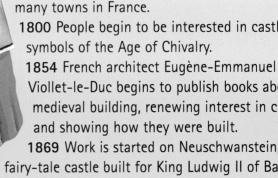

1600 to 2000

1650 Star-shaped forts used to defend many towns in France.
1800 People begin to be interested in castles as symbols of the Age of Chivalry.
1854 French architect Eugène-Emmanuel Viollet-le-Duc begins to publish books about medieval building, renewing interest in castles and showing how they were built.
1869 Work is started on Neuschwanstein, the fairy-tale castle built for King Ludwig II of Bavaria.

Index

Quick-fire Quiz ANSWERS

Page 5 First Knights
1. c 2. a 3. c 4. b

Page 7 Building a Castle
1. a 2. c 3. b 4. b

Page 9 Castle Designs
1. b 2. a 3. b 4. c

Page 11 Parts of the Castle
1. b 2. b 3. c 4. b

Page 13 Castle Life
1. b 2. a 3. c 4. a

Page 15 Becoming a Knight
1. b 2. b 3. a 4. c

Page 17 Heraldry
1. a 2. c 3. c 4. b

Page 19 Horsemanship
1. a 2. c 3. b 4. b

Page 21 Weapons and Fighting
1. c 2. a 3. a 4. b

Page 23 Armor
1. a 2. b 3. c 4. b

Page 25 Siege
1. b 2. b 3. c 4. b

Page 27 Defense
1. b 2. c 3. a 4. a

Page 29 The Crusades
1. b 2. a 3. c 4. a

Page 31 The Knight's Manor
1. c 2. a 3. c 4. c

Page 33 Peacetime Pursuits
1. c 2. b 3. b 4. a

Page 35 Tournaments
1. c 2. b 3. a 4. b

Page 37 The Last Castles
1. c 2. a 3. b 4. b